The Royal Family

The QUEEN

JULIA ADAMS

PowerKiDS press.

Published in 2020 by The Rosen Publishing Group, Inc.
29 East 21st Street, New York, NY 10010

Cataloging-in-Publication Data

Names: Adams, Julia.
Title: The Queen / Julia Adams.
Description: New York : PowerKids Press, 2020. | Series: The royal family | Includes glossary and index.
Identifiers: ISBN 9781725304017 (pbk.) | ISBN 9781725304031 (library bound) | ISBN 9781725304024 (6pack)
Subjects: LCSH: Elizabeth II, Queen of Great Britain, 1926–Juvenile literature. | Queens–Great Britain–Biography–Juvenile literature.
Classification: LCC DA590.A33 2020 | DDC 941.085'092 B–dc23

Editor: Julia Adams
Designer: Rocket Design (East Anglia Ltd)
In-house editor: Sarah Silver

Picture acknowledgements:
Alamy: 10 Granger Historical Picture Archive; 11 Glasshouse Images; 13 (main) Central Press/Stringer; Getty Images: Cover, 8, 18, 22 WPA Pool; 9 Dominic Lipinsky/Stringer; 12 Paul Popper/Popperphoto; 14 (main) Bettman; 15 Chris Ware/Stringer; 16 Hulton Deutsch; 17 (main) Universal History Archive; p. 19 (main) MJ Kim; 21 Luke MacGregor/Stringer; 27 Samir Hussein; iStock: 23 Franckreporter; Shutterstock: 4, 20, 26 Featureflash Photo Agency; 5 Bardocz Peter (modified); 6 Live.Victor; 7 (main) Michael Warwick; 7 (inset) Swapan Photography; 13 (insert) Seeshooteatrepeat; 15 (inset) jalcaraz; 17 (inset) Elina Leonova; 19 (inset) Ed Samuel; 24, 31 Lorna Roberts; 25 (inset) Elayne Massani; 25 (main) Clickmanis; 32 Photo Agency.
All graphic elements courtesy of Shutterstock.

Manufactured in the United States of America

CPSIA Compliance Information: Batch CSPK19: For Further Information contact Rosen Publishing, New York, New York at 1-800-237-9932.

CONTENTS

Who Is Queen Elizabeth?

Elizabeth II is the Queen of the United Kingdom. She is the longest-reigning monarch of the country, having ruled for over 65 years. She represents the UK alongside her husband, Prince Philip, and the royal family.

Head of State

The Queen is the UK's Head of State, which means she is the highest representative of the country, but it doesn't mean that she runs it. At home and abroad, she is the person who acts on behalf of the people in the UK. Elizabeth II is also Head of the Commonwealth – a group of nations who used to be part of the British Empire. Of these, the 15 Commonwealth Realms, such as Canada and Australia, also have her as their Head of State.

Historical reign

Queen Elizabeth is the oldest ruling monarch in the world. During her reign, she has carried out thousands of duties, and greeted millions of people. She is also the most-traveled royal leader in the history of the UK, having visited over 125 different countries by plane, ship, and train. She has even insisted on visiting some states when advised that her life may be in danger, for example because of bomb threats.

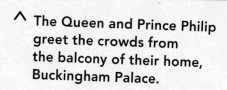

∧ The Queen and Prince Philip greet the crowds from the balcony of their home, Buckingham Palace.

Celebrating with the nation

Over the years, the royal family's celebrations have been marked by people across the UK and abroad. Each royal wedding and birth, as well as the Queen's birthday and jubilees, have been celebrated with street parties, concerts, flotillas and parades. The Queen has joined festivities around the world and hosted international events at her official residences. The 2012 Olympics even saw her take part in a short film starring alongside the famous film character James Bond!

DID YOU KNOW?

* *The Queen speaks fluent French.*

* *The Queen travels abroad without a passport.*

* *During the time of Elizabeth II's reign, 13 UK Prime Ministers, 12 US Presidents, and seven Popes have been in office.*

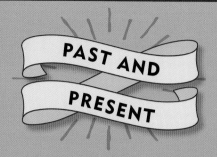

PAST AND PRESENT

THE COMMONWEALTH

In the past, Britain was the center of a worldwide empire, and the British monarch ruled over all the countries in the empire. As many of them became independent, they chose to form a group called the Commonwealth. This allowed them to set up exchange programs, cultural events, such as the Commonwealth Games, and trade deals.

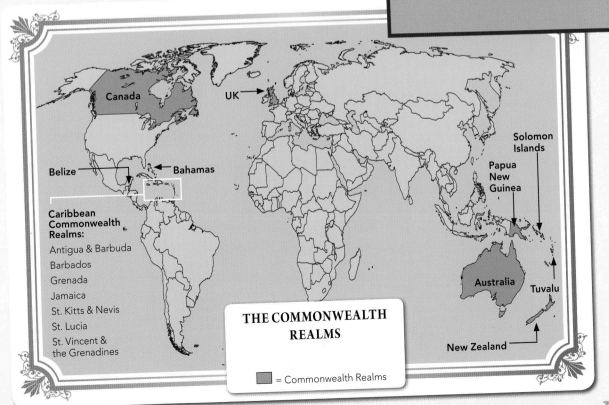

Canada

UK

Solomon Islands

Belize

Bahamas

Papua New Guinea

Caribbean Commonwealth Realms:

Antigua & Barbuda

Barbados

Grenada

Jamaica

St. Kitts & Nevis

St. Lucia

St. Vincent & the Grenadines

Australia

Tuvalu

New Zealand

THE COMMONWEALTH REALMS

▢ = Commonwealth Realms

Royal Power

In the past, the kings and queens of the UK were very powerful. People believed each of them was chosen by God to rule the country, and they were the sole leaders. Nowadays, the role of king or queen is more symbolic, with far less political power.

The Queen and the government

The UK is a democracy. This means that the public vote for the people (politicians) who should run the country. These elected politicians form a government, and the head of the government is the Prime Minister. The Queen talks to the Prime Minister every week, but she has a duty to stay nonpolitical: she doesn't give her opinion on the way the government is running the country.

The Queen and the military

Although the Queen doesn't play a part in deciding when the country goes to war, she is the head of the military, or Commander-in-Chief. This means that every new member of the British Army, the Royal Air Force, and the Royal Marines swears an oath to serve her. She also has ultimate say over how the armed forces are used, but she leaves this decision to the government.

⌄ The Queen's Guard are soldiers from the army who are responsible for keeping the royal family safe and guarding all royal homes.

The Queen and the Church

In 1534, King Henry VIII founded the Church of England, headed by the monarch. Today, the Queen remains the head of the Church, and carries out the appointments of archbishops, bishops, and deans. They, in turn, swear an oath in which they promise to be loyal to the Queen and pay respect to her. The Queen also has a close relationship with the Church of Scotland, though she is not its head.

This is the royal coat of arms for the UK. "ER" stands for "Elizabeth Regina." "Regina" is a Latin word meaning "queen."
∨

FACE OF MANY NATIONS

The Queen's face and coat of arms appear on many official documents in the UK as well as the other Commonwealth Realms. This includes stamps and currency, as well as passports. In her honor, many buildings, bridges, parks, ships, and sports stadiums around the world bear her name.

EUROPEAN UNION
UNITED KINGDOM OF GREAT BRITAIN AND NORTHERN IRELAND

PASSPORT

DIEU·ET· ·MON·DROIT

What Does the Queen Do?

Although the Queen doesn't run the country the way monarchs used to, she still attends many important events throughout the year. She often spends her time off with her family. But what does the Queen do when she is working?

Royal duties

With over 400 engagements a year in her schedule, the Queen is very busy! She holds meetings, called audiences, with officials from other countries. She also attends state visits by foreign leaders, banquets, and openings of important buildings and events. Together with Prince Philip, she has carried out hundreds of overseas visits. She also hosts events called Garden Parties to celebrate the important work people have done in their communities around the country.

∨ The Queen welcomes guests to a Garden Party, hosted at the Palace of Holyroodhouse, Edinburgh.

Investitures

One of the great honors of the Queen is holding investitures. These are events where she presents people with awards for their outstanding services to the country. The awards include Orders of the British Empire, such as Member of the British Empire (MBE) and Officer of the British Empire (OBE), and knighthoods. Male holders of a knighthood are addressed as "Sir" and female ones as "Dame."

Good deeds

Together, the Queen and Prince Philip are patrons of over 1,000 charities. As patrons, they officially support each charity, and will often attend events, such as fundraisers. Given how many charities they support, this takes up a lot of their time, but they feel strongly about each cause and know how much their patronage helps each organization. Over the course of the Queen's reign, the charities she supports have been able to raise approximately $1.8 billion with her help.

ROYAL VISITS

In the past, kings and queens mostly kept their distance from the public. They believed that the monarch's place wasn't with the people, but ruling the country. This changed dramatically under Queen Elizabeth II. Today, she and other members of the royal family often pay visits to people across the country — especially those who have been affected by incredible hardship.

The Queen meeting members of the community of Grenfell Tower in June 2017. Grenfell Tower, an apartment building in west London, was destroyed overnight in a huge fire, leaving many people homeless.

∨

A Princess Is Born

On April 24, 1926, at 2:40 a.m., a baby girl was born who would one day become queen. However, at the time, nobody knew that she would go on to reign over a vast kingdom. She was christened Elizabeth Alexandra Mary.

A growing family

Elizabeth was the first child of the Duke and Duchess of York, and her grandfather was King George V. She was born on Bruton Street, London, and one year later her family moved to Piccadilly, close to her grandparents' home in Buckingham Palace. When Elizabeth was four years old, her sister, Margaret, was born.

Happy childhood

Elizabeth enjoyed looking after her little sister. The princesses grew up in a large house and had nannies who took care of them. They were schooled at home by their governess Miss Marion Crawford, whom they called "Crawfie." Both girls were very close to their parents, and the Duke often referred to the tight-knit family as "us four." But sudden events changed their family life dramatically.

The year of three kings

On January 20, 1936, Elizabeth's grandfather died. It was a great loss for the family, and it also meant that a new ruler needed to be crowned. As King George V's eldest son, Elizabeth's uncle David became King. He was crowned Edward VIII. But, after less than a year, he decided to abdicate, meaning he no longer wanted to be king. The next person in line to the throne was Elizabeth's father, who became King George VI in December 1936.

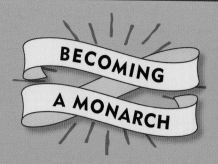

BECOMING A MONARCH

The way someone becomes a king or queen is by being the firstborn. Previously, the crown was passed on to the monarch's eldest son, and only passed on to the eldest daughter if she didn't have brothers. That changed in 2013, when the Queen and the leaders of all Commonwealth Realms agreed to a new law: now, any firstborn, whether a girl or a boy, was first in line to the throne.

< King George VI on the day of his coronation with his wife, Queen Elizabeth, and his daughters, Princess Elizabeth and Princess Margaret.

Future Queen

Nobody had expected King Edward VIII to abdicate, so Elizabeth's family was not prepared to suddenly become the ruling family. When her father became king, Elizabeth, who was then ten years old, knew she would one day become queen.

A new home

As soon as King George VI took to the throne, Elizabeth's family moved to Buckingham Palace. This, along with their new status, was a huge change for them. Suddenly, they were living in a home that had hundreds of rooms, and they no longer enjoyed much of a private life. The princesses weren't allowed to go to the park anymore, or play with children in the neighborhood, because they were now members of the ruling family.

The war

In 1939, the Second World War broke out. Many cities, including London, were bombed regularly, so the royal family moved to the relative safety of Windsor Castle. From there, King George VI traveled to London every day to meet with the Prime Minister and other important politicians. As the war progressed, people had very little access to food and goods, as these were rationed.

Princess Elizabeth, far right, helping out with washing at Girl Guide camp, 1944. Being part of the Girl Guides, similar to Girl Scouts, was a rare occasion for the princesses to spend time with > others their age.

Serving the country

Elizabeth wanted to help in the war effort and be like other children her age. But her father wanted to keep her safe, so he didn't allow her to. When Elizabeth was 14, she and her sister addressed the children of the Commonwealth in a radio speech, expressing their solidarity and compassion. When she was 19, Elizabeth was finally allowed to join the army. She joined a course where she trained as a mechanic and learned how to drive a car. However, she never went to war.

Radio microphone >

Princess Elizabeth > changing the tire of an army vehicle during her military training in 1945.

ROYALS IN SERVICE

Elizabeth was the first female royal in history to receive army training. But she certainly wasn't the first, or last, royal to enter military service. Both her father, King George VI, and her uncle, Edward VIII, served during the First World War. More recently, Queen Elizabeth's grandson, the Duke of Sussex, served on the front line during two tours of duty in Afghanistan.

A Royal Wedding

In 1946, a year after the war had ended, there was exciting news from the royal household: Elizabeth was engaged. She and Philip Mountbatten, a navy officer and son of Greek royalty, had first met seven years earlier. For Elizabeth, it had been love at first sight.

Princess Elizabeth and Philip Mountbatten walk down the aisle of Westminster Abbey on their wedding day. ∨

The ceremony

On November 20, 1947, the royal couple walked down the aisle of Westminster Abbey, in front of over 2,000 invited guests. The country was still recovering from the war, so this was a welcome opportunity to come together and celebrate. Huge crowds lined the streets to cheer on the wedding procession, and over 200 million people worldwide tuned in on their radios to listen to the happy occasion.

In 1947, rationing was still in place. So when the engagement was announced, Elizabeth received ration tokens from well-wishers throughout the country to help her buy the material for her wedding dress.

ROYAL TALK

"I have watched you grow up all those years with pride ... and I can, I know, always count on you, and now Philip, to help us in our work."

Elizabeth's father, George VI, in a letter to his newly married daughter.

A new family

Elizabeth and Philip were now the Duke and Duchess of Edinburgh. The couple's first official tour took them to Paris, France, after which they continued to carry out public duties together. On November 14, 1948, they welcomed a new member to their family: their son Prince Charles Philip Arthur George was born. His sister, Princess Anne Elizabeth Alice Louise, was born two years later, on August 15, 1950. In 1960 and 1964, they were joined by brothers Andrew and Edward.

Royal duties

In 1949, a few months after Charles was born, Philip returned to the navy and was stationed in Malta, so he and Elizabeth were mostly based there, while Charles was looked after at home, in the UK. In 1951, however, the King became sick, and the couple returned to take over some of his duties. They began a royal tour of Australia and New Zealand early the following year, in place of the King and Queen. Their trip started in Kenya, where they stayed in a lodge that had been given to them as a wedding gift.

∧ The royal couple close to their lodge in Kenya on February 5, 1952.

Queen Elizabeth II

Six days into their trip to Kenya, the royal couple were staying in a treetop hotel, observing elephants. It was here that they were contacted with devastating news: the King had died of a heart attack in his sleep. Elizabeth immediately returned home.

Farewell

As soon as her father died, Elizabeth became queen. She landed in London as the new monarch of the country. But before she was crowned, Elizabeth and her family first focused on the preparations for the King's funeral. On February 15, soldiers from the navy drew the King's coffin through London on a carriage. The royal family headed the procession, and thousands of people gathered in the streets to pay their final respects.

Long live the Queen

On June 2, 1953, Elizabeth was crowned Queen Elizabeth II in a grand ceremony at Westminster Abbey. She wore St. Edward's Crown and held a sceptre and orb, which are all part of the priceless Crown Jewels. Her robe was incredibly heavy, so she had prepared for the coronation by practicing at home, walking with bed sheets pinned to her shoulders. Despite the wet weather, huge crowds gathered outside the Abbey to cheer for their new queen.

∧ Queen Elizabeth arrives in England on February 6, 1952, after her father's death. She is greeted by the then Prime Minister, Winston Churchill, and other important politicians.

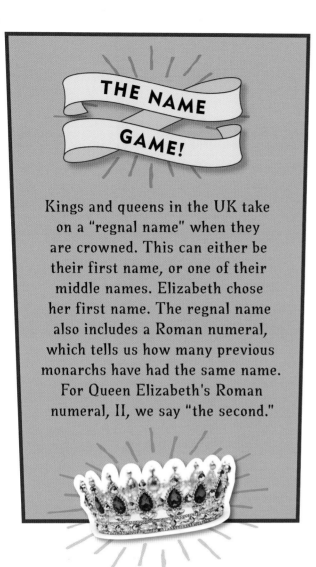

THE NAME GAME!

Kings and queens in the UK take on a "regnal name" when they are crowned. This can either be their first name, or one of their middle names. Elizabeth chose her first name. The regnal name also includes a Roman numeral, which tells us how many previous monarchs have had the same name. For Queen Elizabeth's Roman numeral, II, we say "the second."

Under British law, a woman will take on the title of her husband when she marries, but the same is not true for a man. So even though Elizabeth became queen, Prince Philip did not become king.

TV history

The coronation of Queen Elizabeth II was the first ceremony in the UK to be televised. Many families bought their first TV set specially for the occasion. An incredible 27 million people (of 36 million living in the UK at the time) watched the coronation on TV, while 11 million followed it on the radio. Over 2,000 journalists and 500 photographers from 92 countries covered the event from the streets of London. After a three-hour ceremony, the Archbishop of Canterbury presented the nation with their new queen.

∨ Queen Elizabeth II and the royal family after her coronation. Philip is behind her, the Queen Mother is to the right of her, and her sister, Princess Margaret, is to the left.

Royal Ceremonies

A king or queen's coronation is the most important ceremony in their life, but each monarch takes part in many other regal ceremonies, too. These often consist of centuries-old rituals and customs, and take place every year.

The State Opening of Parliament

Every November, the Queen leads the State Opening of Parliament. This event marks the start of a new year for the British government. After a number of historical rituals have been acted out by Members of Parliament (MPs), the Queen addresses Parliament in the House of Lords. She sits on a golden throne, in regal dress, wearing the Imperial State Crown, and reads out a speech that has been prepared for her.

∨ The Queen opens parliament in 2015. Prince Philip accompanies her, along with her son, Prince Charles, and his wife, Camilla, Duchess of Cornwall.

Remembrance Sunday

On the second Sunday in November, the Queen and her family, along with previous and current members of the armed forces, remember those who have lost their lives in wars and conflicts around the world. They gather by the Cenotaph, a war memorial in London, and when Big Ben strikes 11 a.m. they observe two minutes of silence. Then, each royal lays a wreath of poppies at the foot of the Cenotaph.

TWO BIRTHDAYS?

The Queen celebrates two birthdays — her actual one in April, and an official one in June, which includes a custom called Trooping the Colour. Since 1748, every monarch can choose to have an official birthday that is celebrated in the summer. This is to allow for birthday parades to take place during the warmest time of the year.

< Trooping the Colour, the military parade marking the Queen's official birthday every June. The soldiers are all from the Queen's Household Division. Every year a different troop's flag, or colour, is flown.

Royal Maundy Service

On Maundy Thursday, which is the Thursday before Easter Sunday, the Queen visits a cathedral in the UK to give "Maundy money" to local people. The money is a symbolic amount and is a gift to thank those who have contributed to their community and church. Every person who is given money receives it in two leather purses: a white one and a red one.

The Royal Family

The Queen gets a lot of support in her role from Prince Philip, but also from the rest of her immediate family – her children and grandchildren, as well as their spouses. They all carry out official duties at home and abroad.

∧ Prince Charles attends an awards event for his charity, The Prince's Trust.

The Prince of Wales

As the Queen's eldest son, Prince Charles is the heir to the throne. This means that he sometimes represents his mother at official engagements. As is family tradition, he also carries out a lot of charity work. His own charity, The Prince's Trust, has helped over 800,000 young people find jobs, start their own business or receive professional training. He is very passionate about environmental causes, too, and promotes organic farming and fair trade. He is supported by his wife, Camilla, the Duchess of Cornwall, who also carries out her own charity work.

Royal siblings

Prince Charles's sister and brothers, Princess Anne, Prince Andrew, and Prince Edward, each support hundreds of charities, and attend official events, representing the royal family. In addition, Princess Anne has long been involved with the Olympic Games, first as a competitor in equestrian eventing, and now as President of the British Olympic Association and Member of the International Olympic Committee. She was the director of the team who successfully bid for London to become the host of the Olympic Games 2012.

Princess Anne was the first royal to ever compete in the Olympic Games. She took part in the 1976 Games in Montreal, riding one of the Queen's horses, called Goodwill. She also competed in European championships, winning one gold medal and two silvers.

The next generation

Prince Charles's sons, William and Harry, as well as their wives Kate and Meghan, support the Queen and are dedicated to continuing her work by supporting charities and communities throughout the UK. Together, they run the Royal Foundation, which invests in charities and community causes. Its main focuses are charities for conservation, the armed forces, and young people.

ROYAL TALK

"The monarchy is a force for good, and we want to carry on the positive atmosphere that the Queen has achieved for over 60 years ..."

The Duke of Sussex, Newsweek interview, June 2017

< The Duke and Duchess of Cambridge and The Duke of Sussex with the 2017 London Marathon runners for the mental health campaign Heads Together. The campaign is led by the Royal Foundation and aims to change the way people talk about mental health.

Changing Times

The Queen has been Head of State for over 65 years. During this time, the UK and the rest of the world have changed dramatically. This has even affected royal customs and attitudes, some of which are very different today from when Elizabeth II took to the throne.

The role of the royal family

In the 1950s, the royal family lived a life that was separate from the public in almost every way. They also stuck to many of the ancient royal rituals and customs. Under the Queen's reign, the Royal Household has changed with the times, becoming more open to the public. In the 1990s, the Queen accepted criticism from the public about her privileged lifestyle. In 1993, she started paying tax and set about loosening rules and customs, in order to modernize the household.

^ The Queen warmly greets crowds in Windsor, congratulating her on her 90th birthday. In the past, royals would not have been so close to the public.

Into the digital age

When Elizabeth II was crowned, people were only just starting to buy their first TV sets. There were no cell phones, the internet didn't exist, and photography was still mostly black-and-white. With each technological advance, the royal family have embraced the new possibilities: Buckingham Palace has had a website since 1997, which offers information for tourists and even shows what the royal pets are up to! The royal family is active on all the main social media platforms, offering a glimpse of everyday life as a modern royal.

∧ The royal family has had a Facebook page (called The British Monarchy) since 2010.

Equal rights

Since the 1950s, the rights for many in society have changed for the better. Changes in the law try to ensure that women, the LGBTQ+ community, and ethnic minorities experience equality in the UK. As the UK moves towards becoming a more inclusive society, the Queen tries to reflect this in the Royal Household, as well as the honors she awards as part of the investitures.

The Queen was the first monarch in the world to send an email, in 1976. She was visiting an army base at the time, and the technology was still in its early stages of development.

Royal Homes

Members of the royal family live in historical homes that have housed kings and queens for centuries. Some of these homes are now open to the public.

Buckingham Palace

Located in central London, Buckingham Palace is the main home of the Queen. Here, she hosts state visits, holds some of her annual Garden Parties, and celebrates people's achievements during receptions and investitures. Many family celebrations take place here, including the wedding reception of William and Kate, the Duke and Duchess of Cambridge. Family announcements, such as royal births and deaths, are attached to its front gates for the public to read. During the summer months, part of the palace is open for the public to visit.

Windsor Castle

The Queen spends most of her weekends at Windsor Castle, as well as one month over Easter, called "Easter Court," and a short period in June. When she is "in residence" her flag is flown from the castle's Round Tower. Windsor Castle has been a family home to kings and queens for almost 1,000 years and is the oldest and largest lived-in castle in the world. It was nearly destroyed during a fire in 1992, and it took five years to restore the damage.

∨ The royal family often gathers on Buckingham Palace's famous balcony to greet the public.

Holyroodhouse and Balmoral

When she is in Scotland, the official residence of the Queen is the Palace of Holyroodhouse in Edinburgh. Once a year, at the end of June, she marks "Holyrood Week" during which she and Prince Philip attend events celebrating Scottish culture and history, as well as the achievements of Scottish people from all walks of life. On the rare occasion when the Queen takes time off, she will often retreat to Balmoral Castle, which is like a vacation home for the royal family. The castle looks out over the Scottish Highlands and was built by Queen Victoria and Prince Albert in 1856.

< Balmoral Castle is said to be the Queen's favorite home. She spends time there every summer.

ROYAL PETS

The royal family has a tradition of keeping pets, especially dogs. Queen Elizabeth's father gave her a corgi, named Susan, for her 18th birthday, and she has owned corgis (all descended from Susan) ever since. The Queen also breeds racehorses, who often compete at important equestrian events.

The Future

Even after over 60 years of ruling the country, the Queen remains a busy ruler, fully committed to her role as monarch. But what does the future hold for her and the royal family?

Once Charles becomes king, his wife, Camilla, will become queen. ∧ However, she may go by "Princess Consort" instead of "Queen."

What happens next

When does the Queen's job finish? As with her father, the Queen remains queen until she dies. Some monarchs in other countries have decided to step down early and hand over to their successor, but the Queen has not announced that she plans to do this. Unless she abdicates, the Queen will remain on the throne for the rest of her life. Once she dies, her eldest son, Prince Charles, will become king.

Retirement

Unlike the Queen, Prince Philip has taken a step back from public life and retired in August 2017. This means he remains in his position, but no longer tours the country with his wife, attending events. He also doesn't travel abroad for state visits. The Queen doesn't have this option, but she can choose to attend fewer events, sending other members of the royal family in her place.

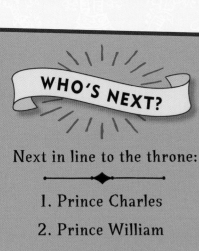

WHO'S NEXT?

Next in line to the throne:

◆

1. Prince Charles

2. Prince William

3. Prince George

4. Princess Charlotte

5. Prince Louis

6. Prince Harry

7. Archie Harrison Mountbatten–Windsor

8. Prince Andrew

9. Princess Beatrice

10. Princess Eugenie

Taking over

Since Prince Philip's decision to retire, Prince Charles has started taking over more leadership duties and accompanies his mother to events around the UK. He has also been taking his father's place when Prince Philip is unwell, such as during the State Opening of Parliament in June 2017. Prince Charles occasionally stands in for his mother, as she gradually hands over royal duties to him. But even at over 90 years old, she remains dedicated to her role and carries out the majority of her duties herself.

The Duke and Duchess of Cambridge with two of their three children, George and Charlotte. The Duke of Cambridge (Prince William), Prince George, Princess Charlotte, and Prince Louis are all in line to the throne. ∨

Kings and Queens of England

The House of Normandy

William I *(William the Conqueror)*	1066–1087
William II *(William Rufus)*	1087–1100
Henry I	1100–1135
Stephen	1135–1154

The House of Plantagenet

Henry II	1154–1189
Richard I *(Richard the Lionheart)*	1189–1199
John	1199–1216
Henry III	1216–1272
Edward I	1272–1307
Edward II	1307–1327
Edward III	1327–1377
Richard II	1377–1399

The House of Lancaster

Henry IV	1399–1413
Henry V	1413–1422
Henry VI	1422–1461

The House of York

Edward IV	1461–1483
Edward V	1483–1483
Richard III	1483–1485

The House of Tudor

Henry VII	1485–1509
Henry VIII	1509–1547
Edward VI	1547–1553
Jane	1553–1553
Mary I	1553–1558
Elizabeth I	1558–1603

The House of Stuart

James I (James VI of Scotland)	1603–1625
Charles I	1625–1649
Commonwealth declared	
Oliver Cromwell Lord Protector	1653–1658
Richard Cromwell Lord Protector	1658–1659
Monarchy restored	
Charles II	1649 *(restored 1660)*–1685
James II *(James VII of Scotland)*	1685–1688
William III and Mary II	1689–1694 (Mary)
	1689–1702 *(William)*
Anne	1702–1714

The House of Hanover

George I	1714–1727
George II	1727–1760
George III	1760–1820
George IV	1820–1830
William IV	1830–1837
Victoria	1837–1901

The House of Saxe-Coburg – becomes House of Windsor in 1917

Edward VII	1901–1910
George V	1910–1936
Edward VIII *(abdicated)*	1936–1936
George VI	1936–1952
Elizabeth II	1952–

The Royal Family Tree

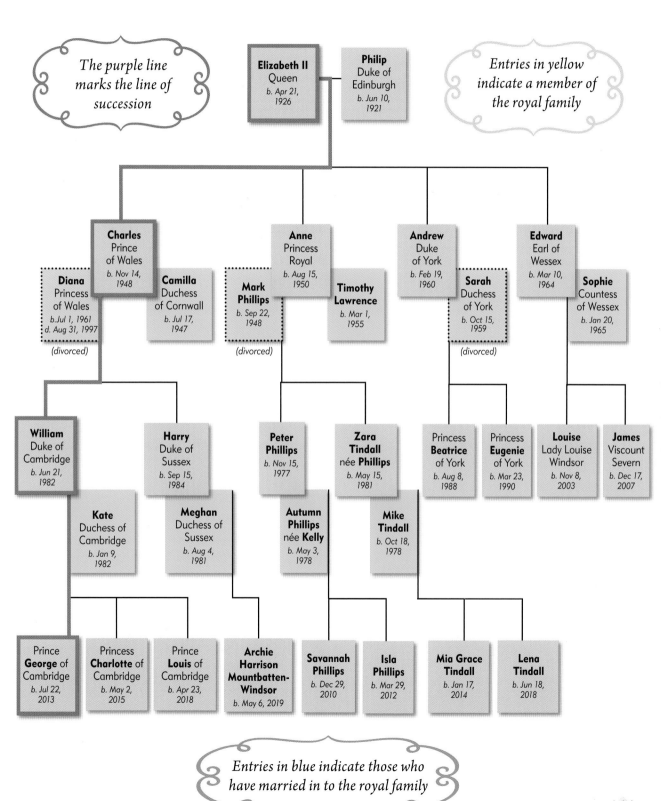

The purple line marks the line of succession

Entries in yellow indicate a member of the royal family

Elizabeth II Queen
b. Apr 21, 1926

Philip Duke of Edinburgh
b. Jun 10, 1921

Charles Prince of Wales
b. Nov 14, 1948

Diana Princess of Wales
b. Jul 1, 1961
d. Aug 31, 1997
(divorced)

Camilla Duchess of Cornwall
b. Jul 17, 1947

Anne Princess Royal
b. Aug 15, 1950

Mark Phillips
b. Sep 22, 1948
(divorced)

Timothy Lawrence
b. Mar 1, 1955

Andrew Duke of York
b. Feb 19, 1960

Sarah Duchess of York
b. Oct 15, 1959
(divorced)

Edward Earl of Wessex
b. Mar 10, 1964

Sophie Countess of Wessex
b. Jan 20, 1965

William Duke of Cambridge
b. Jun 21, 1982

Kate Duchess of Cambridge
b. Jan 9, 1982

Harry Duke of Sussex
b. Sep 15, 1984

Meghan Duchess of Sussex
b. Aug 4, 1981

Peter Phillips
b. Nov 15, 1977

Autumn Phillips née **Kelly**
b. May 3, 1978

Zara Tindall née **Phillips**
b. May 15, 1981

Mike Tindall
b. Oct 18, 1978

Princess **Beatrice** of York
b. Aug 8, 1988

Princess **Eugenie** of York
b. Mar 23, 1990

Louise Lady Louise Windsor
b. Nov 8, 2003

James Viscount Severn
b. Dec 17, 2007

Prince **George** of Cambridge
b. Jul 22, 2013

Princess **Charlotte** of Cambridge
b. May 2, 2015

Prince **Louis** of Cambridge
b. Apr 23, 2018

Archie Harrison Mountbatten-Windsor
b. May 6, 2019

Savannah Phillips
b. Dec 29, 2010

Isla Phillips
b. Mar 29, 2012

Mia Grace Tindall
b. Jan 17, 2014

Lena Tindall
b. Jun 18, 2018

Entries in blue indicate those who have married in to the royal family

29

Glossary

abdicate to give up the throne; to stop being the monarch of a country

British Empire a group of countries that used to be controlled by Britain. The British Empire included countries in North America, the Caribbean, Asia, Africa, and Europe.

coat of arms a symbol that is used by a royal family or a monarch

Commonwealth Realm a Commonwealth country of which the Queen is Head of State

currency the money that is used to pay for goods in a country

equestrian event an event that involves horses, such as a horse race or show jumping

equestrian eventing a combination of different disciplines on horseback, such as show jumping, cross-country, and dressage

flotilla a fleet of ships or boats

front line in war, the front line is the place where the two sides are closest to each other and most of the battle takes place

fundraiser an event that is held to raise money for a charity or other organization

inclusive not excluding (keeping out) anyone; making sure everyone is included

investiture an event at which the Queen awards honors to people, including knighthoods and Orders of the British Empire

jubilee a special anniversary of an event

LGBTQ+ lesbian, gay, bisexual, transgender, queer, and others. These describe a person's sexuality or their gender identity.

oath a solemn promise

patron someone who supports a charity or organization, often with money

ration a fixed amount allowed for one person

regnal name the name a king or queen uses for themselves. It can be different from their birth name, and is followed by a Roman numeral. The numeral counts how many monarchs in history have had the same name.

represent to act on behalf of someone or many people. The Queen represents the UK when she attends events and meetings with leaders from other countries.

spouse a wife or husband

symbolic to represent something or somebody

tour of duty the time that a soldier spends working in a foreign country

Further Information

Books:

Bailey, Jacqui. *Elizabeth II's Reign: Celebrating 60 years of Britain's History.* London, England: Franklin Watts, 2012.

Hansen, Grace. *Queen Elizabeth II: The World's Longest-Reigning Monarch.* Minneapolis, MN: Abdo Kids, 2018.

Manning, Mike, and Brita Granström. *The Story of Britain.* London, England: Franklin Watts, 2016.

Roshell, Starshine. *Real-Life Royalty.* Mankato, MN: Child's World, 2013.

Websites:

The official website of the royal family has details of all its members, as well as royal residences and events such as Trooping the Colour: *www.royal.uk/royal-family*

Visit this page to get an overview of all the British royals, past and present. Click on their portraits to read more about their lives: *www.dkfindout.com/uk/history/kings-and-queens*

Find out more about the Queen by reading these 15 facts: *www.natgeokids.com/uk/discover/history/monarchy/facts-about-the-queen-elizabeth-ii/*

Index